Grandpa, You Have OLD HAIR

Gary Noel

www.ten16press.com - Waukesha, WI

Grandpa, You Have Old Hair
Copyrighted © 2019, 2020 Gary Noel
ISBN 978-1-64538-098-6
Second Edition

Grandpa, You Have Old Hair
by Gary Noel

All Rights Reserved. Written permission must be secured from the publisher to use or reproduce any part of this book, except for brief quotations in critical reviews or articles.

For information, please contact:

www.ten16press.com
Waukesha, WI

Cover design by Kaeley Dunteman

The author has made every effort to ensure that the information within this book was accurate at the time of publication. The author does not assume and hereby disclaims any liability to any party for any loss, damage, or disruption caused by errors or omissions, whether such errors or omissions result from accident, negligence, or any other cause.

To my loving wife, Gail, and our wonderful family. May God continue to bestow his grace and blessings on this special group.

Introduction

"Having children makes you no more a parent than having a piano makes you a pianist." – Michael Levine

"Happiness is having a large, loving, caring, close-knit family – in another city." – George Burns

Webster's New World College Dictionary defines the family as a social unit consisting of parents and the children they rear; the basic unit or primary social group within a culture or society. This definition is lifeless and academic; it lacks energy and feeling. The family is a vibrant, caring, humorous, social experience of a related group of individuals, living their lives and interacting with each other. A good family structure provides love, support and comfort during difficult times and a lot of amusing incidents during other times. So it is with the Noel family. This story is an effort to capture some of the humorous and not so humorous incidents of this special group as they interact with each other and the rest of the world in their travels through life. This is only the starting point, not the completed journey.

The genesis of this project (and coincidentally, the title of this story) is such an incident. Riley, one of our grandsons, and I were walking out of St. Paul's Church together after a Saturday night mass, one week after Christmas, 2007. He looked up at me and, as only a five year old boy would, said, "Grandpa, you have old hair." Somewhat taken aback by his remark because I had no idea what he was talking about or what precipitated his comment, I asked him what he meant by *old hair*? He replied, again void of humor, "Your hair is all gray." That comment broke me up. I didn't have the courage to ask him if he thought I just had old hair, or if it applied to the rest of the body parts, as well. To me it was funny because it was spontaneous and innocent.

After laughing out loud and praising him for his perceptiveness, I repeated the story more than a few times over the next several days. Later, I began to think of the many other humorous incidents and stories we have experienced with our kids that are worth retelling. I decided to recount some of these tales in print for the family enjoyment. When I mentioned my idea to Gail, aka: Hon, Honey, Mom, Gram, or Grandma, she gladly became a collaborator in the project. Immediately we began recalling situations and bantered back and forth about some of these crazy events. One story prompted another story; one event brought to mind a different event. Many of the incidents had been replayed in the past, but more recently have been gathering dust in the recesses of our minds. By the end of the evening, we had so much fun retelling and reliving these incidents, the project had already reaped its first reward.

I hope you enjoy the work half as much as we did developing the material. The grouping of the material is somewhat arbitrary. There is no linear timeline in our memories, so the incidents are packaged in a format that does not follow a particular order or chronology.

Chapter 1: The Dating Game

"That's why guys get married, so they can stop wooing. It's exhausting to woo. You know, you woo, you woo, you woo, and you woo, you gotta go Whoa!" – Paul Reiser

"A man on a date wonders if he'll get lucky. The woman knows." – Monica Piper

Gail and I first met at an after a high school homecoming dance party at the McMullen's house. I was a senior at St. Joe's, an all-boys high school, and she was a junior at Villa Angela, an all-girls high school. Frank, Gail's older brother by one year and my classmate, was hosting the party and several of our high school friends were there. Gail came home after a date and was helping prepare and serve food (yes, even then). We met, but no bells or whistles went off in my brain. A few months later at a Valentine's Day dance at St. Jerome's Church, we met again. Gail and I danced, went to a local restaurant and I took her home. A few chimes faintly tinkled in the recesses of my subconscious. Unaware at the time, that night started our courtship which continues today.

There are always embarrassing events during dating that you wish you could delete and replay the situation with 20/20 hindsight. One such incident occurred early in our courtship. Gail, Frank and I were doing a crossword puzzle on their kitchen table. At that time everything we did was competitive. When Frank read the clue, "a four letter word for a part of the eye," I thought *iris* and blurted out "uterus." Gail's father, who was sitting in the living room reading the newspaper, overheard the comment, came into the kitchen and said, "I had better be there when you look into my daughter's eyes." Without waiting for an explanation from me, he turned and left the room. Frank, who was laughing hysterically at my faux pas, almost fell off his chair at his father's remark. I just sat there, too mortified to say anything. All I could do was turn bright red.

Another memorable moment to forget occurred when I was visiting Gail at Miami of Ohio University. Both Gail and Frank were attending school there. I had taken a Greyhound bus from Cleveland to Oxford to visit Gail for the weekend, and stayed with Frank in his dorm. On Sunday, the students were required to dress up for dinner. For the ladies that meant dresses, or skirts and blouses, and heels or other appropriate footwear; for the men, coats and ties. After the meal Gail and I were walking somewhere on campus when the half-slip she was wearing began to fall. It slid down and ended up around her ankles. (We were walking, scouts honor.) Without missing a beat, she stepped out of the slip, bent down, picked it up and stuffed it in her purse. Instead of making a comforting, romantic or even suggestive remark to relieve the momentary awkwardness, I astutely asked, "What just happened?" Is that creative genius, or what?

Trying to get enough sleep was important for me growing up. I was always looking for ways to sneak in an hour of rest.

It almost proved to be my undoing with my betrothed. After we were engaged, Gail's extended family was having a get-together to welcome me into the group. Somehow I didn't get the message; at least that's my story. I was at home asleep. When I didn't show up after about an hour, Gail called my house (pre-cellphones), and spoke with my mother. When my mom told Gail I was sleeping, Gail asked if she would please wake me up because there was a party going on and I was supposed to be the guest of honor. For whatever reason, my mother was reluctant to disturb me and told Gail I had just fallen asleep a short time ago. Gail was insistent. My mom finally capitulated and woke me. I dressed quickly and left for the party. I don't recall if Gail even talked to me the rest of the night, but she was certainly upset with her sleep-deprived, absent fiancé.

Chapter 2: The Begats

"Adam was one hundred and thirty years old when he begat a son in his likeness…and named him Seth. Adam lived eight hundred years after the birth of Seth and he had other sons and daughters." – Gen: 5:3

Gary and Gail begat Gary, Greg, Terri, Kristin, Brian and Steven. (Can you imagine what the zero population crowd would say about these two if they remained prolific for eight hundred years???)

Christmas 1967 was the first Christmas in two years we were together as a family. Gary was twenty months and Greg was six months old. I was still in the Army, but stateside after a thirteen month overseas separation. We were stationed at Ft. Eustis, Virginia, home of the Army Transportation Corps. For some unexplained reason, my military pay stopped when I returned from overseas and I had not been paid for three months. Consequently, it was going to be a very lean Christmas. Ed and Donna Gerhold wanted to get together with us for Christmas dinner and they offered to bring the food. Ed was my roommate for part of the time while I was in Korea and we became good friends. He was also stationed at Ft. Eustis. It was a gracious offer, consistent with the true meaning of the holiday.

Ed and Donna did not have any children at that time,

but they had two Siamese cats (who thankfully stayed at their apartment.) Between our two boys, Donna favored Gary because Greg was too active for her. After a round of holiday cheer and some friendly conversation, we sat down for dinner. Gail had set the table with a linen table cloth, napkins and china I had bought in Korea. Gary was in a high chair at the table and Greg was in a playpen right next to the table. I am not sure if Greg resented being in the playpen, was trying to improve his standing with Donna, or he was foreshadowing his later baseball prowess, but he sure captured the moment. While we were eating, he picked up a soft rubber ball about the size of a softball from the playpen and threw it at the table. The ball landed directly in the gravy boat and sent gravy flying everywhere. He certainly didn't improve his status with Donna with that move. Although I didn't say anything at that time, I was amazed at the accuracy of the throw.

Washington, DC was the location for two memorable events in our lives. The first one occurred in April, 1968. I briefly considered staying in the Army (yes, they did finally start paying me again) for an additional three years if I could go to grad school and get an MBA while on active duty. Gail was not quite on board with this plan, but she was willing to at least see what the Army had in mind for her husband if he stayed in the military. Ed Gerhold was considering a career in the military. Both of us made appointments with the Transportation Corps Personnel Section in Washington, DC to explore our future options in the Army. Keep in mind this was early in 1968 during the height of the Vietnam War.

Our wives and Gary, who was almost two, joined us on the

trip. A neighbor offered to watch Greg, so we planned to spend the day in DC sightseeing after our morning appointments. Gail, Gary and I were up early and left our apartment before 6:00 a.m. since it was about a two hour trip from Ft. Eustis to the Pentagon. We had not listened to the news the night before (the late news starts at 11:00 p.m. on the east coast). When we picked up Ed and Donna, they shocked us with the news that Martin Luther King had been assassinated in Memphis, Tennessee. Stunned with the news, we speculated how this event would affect the mood of the country already besieged with many other controversies, not the least of which was the Vietnam War. So engrossed in our own conversations, we barely listened to the radio on the way to DC.

    Our meetings lasted less than fifteen minutes each. Both of us were told if we continued in the Army, our next duty station would be Vietnam. There were no other options. Since neither of us was anxious to complete another short term tour of duty (at least another twelve months) without our families, there was no further discussion about staying in the Army.

    By the time we rejoined our wives and Gary mid-morning, the city had erupted in chaos. Rioting was occurring all over the DC area. Government offices were closing, and everyone was advised to get out of the city. We decided to forego the sightseeing and head back to Ft. Eustis. As soon as we left the Pentagon, we encountered six lanes of bumper-to-bumper traffic and very little movement. As we were sitting trapped in traffic with no place to go, we saw a group of thugs pile out of a car, smash all the street-side windows of a huge downtown department store with baseball bats, grab everything out of the window displays, including the mannequins, run down the street and vanish around the corner. According to radio reports, looting and burning were occurring throughout the city. Although we did not experience any more lawlessness first hand, we were concerned about our safety and anxious to get out of the city.

When we finally arrived back at our apartment after a long and hectic day, our neighbor was waiting for us with Greg and the news that someone from my battalion headquarters had called several times during the day trying to get a hold of me. I immediately called the duty desk and found out our unit was on active alert for riot duty. I had to pack and get to the base as quickly as possible. We were going to the DC area! That event considerably predated the current saying, "Been there, done that."

After surviving the riots and the remaining few months on active duty, we were more than ready to return to civilian life. It is a military tradition that active duty personnel can "sign out" from their unit's military roster any time after midnight on the last day of active duty. With a very pregnant (eight months) Gail, and three kids (Gary, Greg, and Ray, Gail's twelve year old brother, who had been staying with us for a few weeks) in the car, I drove to our battalion headquarters on final time around 12:45 a.m. and officially ended my active duty obligation. Every available inch in our car was packed with essentials we would need until our household goods shipment arrived back in Ohio. On the way out the gate, I returned the salute from the MP on duty one final time, and we bid Ft. Eustis and the Army life good-bye and headed north.

I missed a turn on one of the main streets to take us on a freeway around Washington, DC (pre Google maps) and ended up hopelessly lost in the middle of a burned out area in DC around 3 a.m. When I finally saw a police car, I pulled up behind it, flashed my headlights and got out of the car to ask the policeman for directions out of town. After his opening comment about what in the hell was I doing in this part of the city at this time, he tried to give me directions. Finally, he must have seen my concern and the anxious looks from the kids pressed against the windows, he told me to get back into my car, lock the doors and follow him. He cautioned us against stopping for anyone or anything. He led us out of the city and back to the correct freeway. Finally, he pulled off to the side of the road, lowered his window and pointed to the entrance of the expressway we needed. As we passed, he gave us a final, good luck wave. We gratefully returned the wave as we headed north again. I don't know what, if anything, he put in his duty log about the lost, distraught family, but he was certainly an angel of mercy for us that night.

Before leaving the journey from Virginia to Ohio, I have to mention one more incident en route. It may sound humorous now, but, I can assure you, it was not funny at the time. Keep in mind the car (a sedan, not a minivan) was packed so tight, there was barely enough room for the five of us. I had a porta-crib wedged in the back seat for Gary and Greg, and just enough room next to it for Ray. Several necessities were stuffed around the kids and other items were jammed on the floor and under the front seat. To say we were crowded would be an understatement.

We drove all night and reached the Pennsylvania turnpike early in the morning. The three kids were sleeping. As it grew lighter, Gail and I became more excited about returning home and beginning our new lives together. Suddenly Ray, who was prone to car sickness, woke up and said he felt like he was going to throw up. Since we were on the turnpike without any immediate place to stop, I told him to roll down the back window, stick his head out and get some fresh air. The next thing we heard was the unmistakable sound of someone heaving. Ray proceeded to deposit his last three meals all over the inside of the back seat and the two boys who were sleeping in the crib next to him. The whole car suddenly reeked! Remember, Gail was eight months pregnant. I quickly pulled over on the shoulder of the turnpike, ran around the car and helped Ray out as cars were passing us going well in excess of the sixty miles per hour speed limit. When I asked him why he didn't lean his head out the window when he knew he was going to be sick, he told me he didn't want to throw up on the car behind us. Sometimes, thinking of others can be overrated.

Having a generous nature is a trait often compensated in unanticipated ways (such as meeting your future wife because you stopped to ask a young lady if she needed help moving into her apartment). However, there are other times when generosity is not so aptly rewarded. When Gary was four, he decided to give his sister, Terri, a special Easter present. Several days before the blessed event, he wrapped three of his keepsake stones and planned to give them to her on Easter morning. Brimming with the feeling that it is better to give than receive, he repeatedly told Terri he had a special present for her and she would be so happy when she opened the gift. When the big day finally arrived and Terri's expectations were sky high, he proudly handed her his gift. As Terri opened the wrapping, she didn't act like someone who had been given a treasured keepsake. She shrieked with disappointment, "These are just dumb old rocks!" Then she began to cry. Gary was crushed.

Staying with the gift theme, Steven also liked to give special gifts. Not having much money at a young age, he developed a skill for re-gifting. Not quite as generous as Gary, he wouldn't give away his prized possessions to someone else. Rather, he would rummage around, grab something that already belonged to the person he was giving the gift, usually his mom, wrap it up in old newspaper (he was frugal, even then) and proudly give it to that person. He didn't even need a special day like a birthday, anniversary or Christmas. He would create his own celebration. It might be the second Tuesday of the month, or the fifth snow fall of the season. Those "treasured" items included bars of soap (only slightly used), deodorant (always a favorite), shaving cream, half empty bottles of perfume, boxes of Jell-O and other random things.

Gary and Terri were the principal players in another classic family drama. In order to fully appreciate the tale, the reader has to understand the setting. The first home we lived in when we returned to Euclid from the military was a small, rented cottage on the shores of Lake Erie. As the scene opens, Mom is in a tiny crawl space in the boys' bedroom looking for change of season clothing for the kids. Gary (about four) comes running into the room, yelling that Terri is crying. Mom, knowing the two of them were playing in her bedroom, shouts that she will be there in a minute, and suggests Gary give Terri a balloon to see if that will quiet her. (I am not sure where the balloon came from, but it was an essential prop for the rest of the story.) Gary proceeds to run back to the other bedroom and gives Terri a balloon. Two minutes later, he comes running back and tells Mom he gave Terri the balloon, but she's still bleeding. That was a show stopper! Mom immediately forgets about the clothes and rushes into her room. She discovers Terri had been jumping on our bed and hit her forehead on the headboard. (Apparently we had not told Terri about what the doctor said to the monkeys who were jumping on the bed.) A quick trip to the hospital and seven stiches later, everything was back to normal.

Shadowing is a technique for high school and early college students to get exposure to certain professions or occupations. Terri had her own version of this process, total immersion. Perhaps foreshadowing her career as a nurse, she spent a bit of time in hospitals. Her initial stay after her birth was during her first Christmas holidays. After a seemingly normal five months (aside from her colic episodes) Terri suddenly became very lethargic and listless. Obviously concerned over what was happening to her previously active baby, Gail got an immediate appointment with our pediatrician. After a thorough exam, the doctor had no idea what was wrong and recommended we take Terri to Babies and Children's Hospital in Cleveland for further testing. When a blood test turned up nothing, she was admitted for further testing. After a few more swings and misses, one of the doctors examining her advised a spinal tap to see if there was anything in her spinal fluid to help clear up the mystery.

Both Gail and I were frantic over the way things were going. While this testing was going on, each of us were interrogated separately to determine if there was physical abuse in the house. We were upset by these questions, implying that one or both of us had abused our five-month-old daughter, but understood the doctors were grasping at anything. Finally, after about three days, Terri began to recover and again became an active baby. We took her home, but never received a precise diagnosis of the problem. The doctors surmised either she had a severe reaction to the medicine she was taking for colic, or she somehow had an allergic reaction to the Christmas tree. Another hospital immersion to come.

The first house we owned was a cute, small bungalow (less than 1,000 square feet) on Farringdon Avenue in Euclid, Ohio. The house had no basement and very limited storage, but we were proud of our first home. There were three bedrooms, the master bedroom on the main floor and two upstairs. The boys shared one and Terri's bedroom doubled as a playroom. The house was approximately ½ mile from Grandma Ray's house, also on Farringdon, but across a very busy E. 260th street. One morning Gail was talking to her mom on the phone about picking up her waffle iron because she was planning on making waffles. About fifteen minutes later, Grandma called Gail back to ask why Kristin was at her house. Kristin was three at the time. Unbeknown to her mom, Kristin had overheard the conversation about picking up the waffle iron and decided to get it herself. She walked from our house to Grandma's house, across the busy street, to save her mom a trip. Even at that young age, Kristin was thinking of others. Needless to say, she did not walk back by herself.

On another occasion, Gail was driving from our house to her mom's with Kristin and Brian in the back seat. This was pre-seat belts. The car she was driving had been hit recently in the back passenger door, so the door did not always close completely. The two sides of Farringdon did not line up directly opposite one another. In order to go from our side of Farringdon to the other side, you had to turn right onto 260th and then make a quick left back onto Farringdon. As Gail was maneuvering through the turns (a move she had made hundreds of times), the back door swung open and Brian tumbled out of the car onto the street. Fortunately, the driver of the car heading directly for Brian had seen what had happened, stopped and beeped his horn. Then he jumped out of his car and stopped traffic. Hearing the honking and Kristin screaming, Gail turned and saw the back door opened and no Brian. She immediately stopped, leaped out of the car, ran back and picked up Brian, who was lying in the middle of the street, crying. Other than a few scrapes from hitting the pavement, Brian was not injured. To this day, Brian claims he remembers falling out of the car, even though he was only eighteen months old.

Speaking of our first house (and maybe a bit of foreshadowing of my later job with Spancrete), the front walk was broken and uneven. It was probably twelve feet long and three feet wide from the drive to the front door. At some point, we decided to dig out the old walk and replace it with new concrete. Keep in mind we had never so much as patched a crack in concrete.

After reading a do-it-yourself manual on how to pour a concrete walk, we laboriously dug out the old walk, leveled the ground as best we could with hand tools, and framed the area with 2x 4's for the new walkway. Next, we rented the smallest and cheapest cement truck (yes, a cement truck) we could find and ordered a small load of concrete. I am not sure what methodology we used to calculate the amount of concrete we would need, but we badly miscalculated and had enough concrete to pour a driveway in addition to the walkway.

Also, when ordering the truck, I neglected to specify I wanted one with adequate brakes to stop the truck with a load of concrete. I discovered my error after I pulled onto the street. Even though it was a small cement truck, it was still a cement truck with a rolling drum full of concrete! The first time I tried to stop, the brake pedal plunged all the way to the floor with very little impact on my speed. Fortunately, the truck had a standard transmission, so I began feverishly down shifting to slow the truck down. I didn't hit anything, but I don't think I went more than ten miles per hour the rest of the way home. That created another problem since we had rented the truck for only four hours. By the time I got to our house and parked the truck in the drive, I was emotionally drained and had used up a significant portion of the four hours.

Next, we had to unload the concrete from the truck to a wheelbarrow and then to the walkway. My primary helpers were Ray, age 14, Gary, age 6, and Greg, age 5. All three boys had on old clothes and wore oversized gloves and safety glasses. They looked like rejects from the Little Rascals. Gail was the reader of the "How To Do It" manual. Somehow, we managed to keep the mixture somewhat liquid and move enough of it from the truck to fill up the area we dug out without making too much of mess in the driveway. After partially filling the cavity with concrete, we now had to begin finishing the surface before it hardened. I had borrowed some concrete finishing tools, but I never attempted to finish concrete prior to that job. Also, with the warm, sunny afternoon, the concrete began to firm up more quickly than I had anticipated. So I had to begin the finishing process while still continuing to pour. (Does the phrase "busier than a one armed paper hanger" come to mind?) If anyone watched us working that day, they would have thought we were auditioning for a Three Stooges movie.

During the entire process of pouring and finishing, I had this sickening feeling that I had to return this truck, still partially loaded, back to the rental yard. If I had not left our car at the yard, I would have called and told them to come and get their brakeless truck. God must have been smiling at the ineptitude of this small band of "construction workers" that afternoon and provided some special guidance, because we were able to complete the job and return the truck without any further incident.

In spite of our inexperience, the walk ended up looking fairly level and presentable, except for the imperfections on each the side of the walk. When I attempted to remove the framing from the concrete after it had hardened, there was considerable flaking and chipping on the edges. I must have skipped the part in the manual about oiling the inside of the boards to seal them so the newly poured concrete would not adhere to them when the boards were removed. After backfilling with dirt and planting grass right to the edges, the flaws weren't that noticeable and the project was considered a success.

Another unusual, almost tragic incident, took place shortly after we moved into the house on Farringdon. We were the last house on the north side of Farringdon. The house next to us to the east was the first house facing 266th street. The Jenson family lived in that house. Mr. and Mrs. Kochenmeister, a couple in their eighties (not quite as old now as it seemed then), lived in the house next to the Jenson's. Our backyards were separated by a white, wood picket fence. Our three older kids were fond of Mrs. Kookie, and we often shared neighborly chats over the four foot high fence.

Often, on warm, sunny afternoons in the late spring and summer, Mrs. Kookie would relax in a lawn chair on her driveway, in front of her garage. The garage was not attached to the house, but set back approximately thirty feet. On this particular day, she was sitting in front of her garage just enjoying the sunshine. Gary and Greg were playing ball in our backyard. When the ball went over the fence and landed in her yard, Gary, who was five at the time, called to her and asked if she would get their ball. She slowly got out of her chair and ambled over to the ball.

At that very instant, a car drove through a stop sign opposite her house and roared straight up her driveway. It crushed the lawn chair she had been sitting in, crashed through the closed garage door, and came to rest half way through the back end of the garage. The driver of the car was a sixteen year old who had his driver's license for one week. His foot either slipped off the brake and hit the accelerator, or hit the accelerator instead of the brake. Either way, the result was chaos. He hit the garage door with such force that the car went all the way through the garage and half way out the back. He pushed the back of the structure into our yard, collapsing the fence and missing our house, and the room baby Kristin was napping in, by less than three feet.

Mr. Kookie came hobbling out the side door of their house, pulling up his pants. We found out later he was in the bathroom when he heard the crash. After looking at the garage and realizing what had just happened, he simply stared at the devastation. When he saw his wife coming from the back yard, he almost started to cry.

The young driver was able to shove open his car door and walk out of the garage. He appeared unhurt, but was almost crying he was so upset about what had happened. He apologized over and over again. Had Gary not called Mrs. Kookie to retrieve the ball, she would have been in the direct line of the car that smashed her garage. I guess there is something to be said for the old baseball adage, you should always back up every throw, even if you are an elderly woman.

Chapter 3: On Wisconsin, On Wisconsin...

*"Moving on is a simple thing,
what it leaves behind is hard." – David Mustaine*

"It's interesting to leave a place, interesting even to think about it. Leaving reminds us of what we can part with and what we can't, then offers us something new to look forward to, to dream about."
– Richard Ford

After working for Euclid, Inc., and its parent, White Motor Corporation, for almost eight years, it was time for a job change. The corporation was facing bankruptcy and jobs were being eliminated. An on again, off again merger with another local company held little prospect for the future. I began interviewing, hoping to find something in the greater Cleveland area. Nothing suitable materialized. I expanded the scope of my search to the Midwest. After a series of interviews with Koehring Company, I was offered a position as Human Resources Manager for their largest division. Unfortunately, the company and the division were located in Milwaukee, Wisconsin. After some difficult discussions about the future and separating from both our families, we decided to accept the offer.

Moving to Wisconsin in 1976 meant uprooting our

immediate family and leaving behind our extended family. It was particularly difficult for Gail because she was leaving her widowed mother, two younger brothers and sister. The four of them had been an intimate part of our family for many years. Gail, Gary and Greg lived with Grandma Ray while I was in Korea. We lived with them for a few months after we came back from the service. Then we rented a house (actually it was a cottage) within five minutes of their home. When we bought our first home, it was on the same street as Gail's mom.

Gail talked to her mother and her siblings daily. We were together for dinner probably five nights out of seven, and we played bridge with Grandma and Ray on many weekends. My parents, my sister, brother-in-law and their large family, and my older brother also lived in the area. When we weren't with Gail's family, we often were with my family. We knew all this would change with the move. Despite the promise that we would visit often, our lives would be very different going forward. To counter those difficult issues, we would be moving to a new, more secure, job, a new home (not brand new, but new to us), new adventures and a new life in the Badger state. But, we were leaving both of our families and all our friends for an unknown future.

We did drive back to Ohio at least three times a year for many years, enduring the Chicago traffic both going and coming. We always went back at Christmas time, at least once during the summer, and on many other special occasions. Most of the trips were uneventful, but there were a few memorable ones.

On one such trip, we were returning to Wisconsin on New Year's Eve day. The weather forecast was for snow later in the day in western Indiana and the Chicago area. We left Grandma

Ray's house early in the afternoon with the sun shining and the temperature in the low fifties. We stopped in Fremont, Ohio, not too far out of our way home, to visit Uncle Adam and Aunt Donna. In retrospect, that was a HUGE tactical error. After visiting for a few hours, we resumed our trip west around 4 p.m.

It started to snow around South Bend and intensified as we drove through the western part of Indiana. Snow began to accumulate on the turnpike. As we entered Illinois, the weather bureau was forecasting blizzard conditions for the greater Chicago area, and advised only emergency vehicles should be on the roads. We were more than three hours from home and talked about alternative plans. If it wasn't New Year's Eve, we would have headed to the nearest motel and ridden out the storm in safety. However, both Gail and I were concerned that we might have difficulty finding a vacancy and would be wasting precious time in our search.

After agonizing over the possibility we could get stuck on the freeway or end up in a snow bank somewhere, we decided to keep going, despite the ominous forecast and the heavy snow. Chicago was shutting down all around us. We had never encountered as little traffic driving through Chicago as we did that night. I stayed in the tire tracks of cars ahead of us and did a lot of praying. Visibility was extremely limited. At one point, the only vehicle we could see was a snow plow. I tried to stay reasonably close to it, so we could continue driving on a plowed highway.

Somehow, we got through Chicago and into Wisconsin. By this time, there wasn't anyone else on the road. The freeway was snow covered, but still drivable. Because most sane people had heeded the warnings and stayed off the roads, the plows were effective in keeping the interstate passable. Midnight came and went without a great deal of celebrating in our car.

When we finally exited the freeway in Waukesha, we gave a great sigh of relief for making it this far, but we didn't know what to expect next. We had made it from Cleveland to Waukesha through the brunt of the storm, but we still had ten miles or so to go on unplowed city streets before we reached home. The weather had been in the sixties when we left Wisconsin on Christmas day, so we didn't have any boots or warm clothing with us in the car. Parking the car in some parking lot or abandoning it on the side of the road, and trying to walk the rest of the distance was not a realistic option. Besides, it was after three in the morning.

Adrenaline had kicked in hours ago and was starting to wane. I continued to drive slowly and cautiously, but kept moving forward. Finally, we made it to our street. After all we had been through, I was determined to reach our driveway despite the amount of snow all around us. I got the car off the street and halfway up our driveway, so the plow could get by in the morning. After more than thirteen hours of exhaustive driving, we had arrived home safely. We unloaded the essential things from the car and headed into the house. Home never felt so good!

On another return trip from Ohio, this time in the summer, we had car problems. It was a late Sunday afternoon and the temperature was still close to ninety. Traffic around Chicago was heavy and slow. The radiator in our six year old station wagon decided it couldn't handle the weather any longer and overheated. Steam billowed out from the front of the car and the emergency light flashed on the dashboard. We had to stop on the inside shoulder on the Dan Ryan Expressway. The mood inside the wagon sank to near desperation. For the uninitiated, the Dan Ryan runs by Chicago's south side, possibly the toughest area in the entire city. It is not the type of neighborhood where an outsider could knock on a stranger's door and ask for some water.

After sitting for more than twenty minutes while the engine cooled and tempers flared, we tried to talk somewhat rationally about our options. The most favorable, in my opinion, was having one of Chicago's finest stop, check out the problem, and provide us with some water. I'm not sure where I thought they were going to get the water, but I was hopeful. The older boys, Gary and Greg, half-heartedly volunteered to walk somewhere to try and get help, hoping one or both parents would decline their offer. Gail was as anxious as the rest of us to get out of there, but vetoed their suggestion, not willing to sacrifice her two oldest sons at the altar of desperation. Terri, the surprising optimist, was sure another motorist would stop and lend a helping hand. She was so convinced that she made a sign and held it in the window. The sign read, "H2O needed." Other than a few crude comments by passersby, no one offered assistance. Apparently, not too many of the drivers passing us had taken a high school chemistry class and understood the problem.

Keep in mind this was pre-cell phone era. We had no means of communication with anyone. Finally, after sitting there for more than thirty minutes, a car pulled over on the shoulder in front of us and the driver asked if we needed help. When I explained the problem, he offered us two gallon containers of water that he had in his car. For the unbelievers, how do you explain why that car, which happened to have two gallon jugs of water, decided to stop and offer help? Since our engine had cooled sufficiently,

I was able to fill the radiator with the water, start the car and drive to the Lake Forrest Oasis, the last major stopping point in Illinois, and a much friendlier environment. The radiator had a leak and whenever the engine stopped and the pressure was off, all the water leaked out. After the necessary pit stop, we again filled the radiator with water, using the same containers the Good Samaritan had given us, and successfully finished the trip to Waukesha. The next day I made an appointment with our local mechanic to fix the radiator

Unfortunately, I didn't get the name of the stranger who helped us, so I was never able to thank him formally for his kindness. I'm sure he will be rewarded for his good deed.

Chapter 4: Family Vacations/Outings

"The rainy days a man saves for usually seem to arrive during his vacation." – Author Unknown

"Those that say you can't take it with you never saw a car packed for a vacation trip." – Author Unknown

Family vacations/outings are unique opportunities to create special memories that will remain for a lifetime. The assumption is the memories will be positive ones. Reality often intervenes and establishes its own criteria. We have experienced several memorable vacation moments. (I'll leave it up to the reader to decide if they were positive ones.)

How can we forget the time Gail and I went away for our first weekend alone after returning from the Army? We made reservations at the Historic Summit Inn in rustic, western Pennsylvania, a place my parents had recommended. In hindsight, I should have asked them if there was an age requirement (as in, only over sixty need apply). Grandma Ray babysat for our three kids, and we left on a Friday with high expectations for a weekend filled with fun and romance.

This place, built in 1907, may have been an enjoyable vacation resort in the thirties and forties, but by the early seventies it was more like a tired old age home. They actually served tea and cookies in the afternoon. We were the youngest couple in the whole place (by at least fifty years). The most exciting activity during our visit was a shuffleboard tournament. Our room looked like it belonged in Gail's Grandmother's house, right down to the chenille bedspread and the rocking chair. The door to our room was warped and could not close properly; the floor was uneven and creaked whenever we walked on it. The only redeeming factor was that we were together, by ourselves, for three days. There was not a second annual visit to the Historic Summit Inn.

We should have taken that trip as some kind of omen regarding vacations, but, undeterred, we continued to persevere. When I was working for White Motor Corporation, I had a chance to use a recreational vehicle free for a three day weekend. At that time, White Motor had a small division in Michigan that manufactured recreational vehicles. This particular thirty-one foot RV was a "demo" based in Cleveland. When the Sales Department wasn't using it, executives at the Corporate Office could sign up for it. Apparently, someone cancelled at the last minute, and my boss asked me if I would be interested in using it for the next three days. I agreed immediately, and in less than two hours Gail and I put together a trip for our five kids and Mary, Gail's fourteen year old sister. We planned to drive to Hueston Woods State Park, a popular camping area in southern Ohio, near Oxford, and spend the night. The next day we wanted to visit the Miami of Ohio campus and show the kids where their mom went to college. The highlight of the trip was to be on Sunday, a visit to King's Island Amusement Park.

The Friday morning of our big trip, I was at work and received a call from my former boss, telling me Gail's mom had just been terminated from her job as a correspondent in the Parts Department. I was upset at the decision and concerned about Gail's mom, but I was furious that no one from the that department, a personnel department I had worked in for more than four years, had the courtesy to call and give me a heads up before it happened. I immediately called Gail to let her know. We considered not going on the trip, but after we spent some time with her mom, she begged us to go. We didn't leave until late afternoon. Our collective moods were less than upbeat. By the time we reached Hueston Woods, it was midnight and the campground was totally dark. We couldn't find our campsite, and after driving around the campgrounds twice and disturbing many of the other campers, we just parked for the night at a vacant site.

The next day we had breakfast in the RV and then drove to Miami of Ohio. The campus covers more than 2,000 acres and most of the buildings are built in the Georgian Revival architectural style. It is an impressive setting. The college was once described by poet Robert Frost as "the most beautiful campus ever there was." At their ages, I'm not sure our kids appreciated the aesthetics, but they did enjoy visiting a dorm and seeing where their mom had gone to school.

During one of the stops, two year old Kristin tripped getting out of the vehicle, hit her head on the hand railing, and stumbled onto the ground. She cut herself just below her eyebrow and screamed to let us know she was hurting. Gail stopped the bleeding with a cloth and tried to settle her down.

While Gail was tending to Kristin, I grabbed a bandage and fashioned a butterfly binding to close the wound. We debated whether or not to take her to an emergency room for a stitch or two. Kristin was definitely not in favor of that plan. Gail and I finally decided not to go the hospital route, primarily because we didn't know where to find one, and the bandage seemed to be holding the cut closed. Kristin was relieved, but she still has a tiny scar above the corner of her right eye as a permanent memento of that trip.

On Sunday morning, I got lost (a recurring theme throughout our marriage) driving through the northern Kentucky hills on our way to church. I was speeding, trying to make up time. Gail was doing her hair, trying to get ready and assisting me with directions. Brian, who was about seven months old, started to cry. When Gail got up to try and help him, I swerved the RV going around a bend and she landed in a partially filled diaper container. After a few choice words about the driver, she extracted herself from the pungent pail, wiped herself off, and continued on her rescue mission to help Brian.

That set the tempo for the rest of the day. After church, we went to King's Island, the amusement park that was supposed to be the highlight of the trip. It was already in the mid-nineties by the early afternoon. After going on a few rides, the complaints about the heat started. No one felt like standing in long lines in the sun, waiting for their turn. Gail had prepared some sandwiches, so we decided to find some shade and have something to eat. After lunch Greg and the other kids were standing in line for another ride when he got sick and threw up all over himself. Fortunately, no one else was similarly afflicted. After getting him cleaned up, we decided to cut the park visit short, and left a short time later.

On the way back home, a cold front must have passed through the area. The wind picked up and it began to rain. After about two hours of a five hour trip, the rain became monsoon-like and the wind was really howling. Being an inexperienced RV driver, I was struggling to keep the vehicle on the interstate. I had just asked Gail to look for a spot where I could get off the freeway when, without warning, the bottom of the windshield blew off its track and the middle bowed inward toward us about three inches. With the rain pounded against the window and the wipers no longer effective, I could barely see. The water started pouring through the opening. I was afraid the whole windshield was about to shatter. With my vision blurred, I struggled to maintain control of the vehicle and, as quickly as I could, pulled over to the side of the road. After coming to a stop, I momentarily sat frozen at the wheel. The growing stream of water flowing down the instrument panel snapped me back to reality. Gail yelled for the kids to grab some towels. She started to wipe up the water. Then she and I carefully, and I repeat ever so carefully, used the towels to push the front window back in place. When it snapped into its track, we breathed a sigh of relief and finished mopping up the rest of the water.

Without any means of communication (remember, pre-cell phone era), we sat there a long time, hoping the storm would subside. After repeated questions from the older kids about what were we going to do, the very question I was wrestling with, I tried to sound confident about the next move. As calmly as I could, without revealing my inner turmoil, I told them we would resume as soon as the wind and rain slowed down. They quickly sensed the real concern, and asked if the windshield was going to stay in place. With false bravado, I assured them there was nothing to worry about now that we had it back in its track. Eventually the rain did slow and the wind became less of a factor, so we decided to give it a try. First, we packed the inside bottom of the windshield with the already damp towels in an attempt to hold everything in place and prevent any more water from seeping onto the dash After a quick prayer to St. Christopher, the patron saint of travelers, we began to white-knuckle it the rest of the way. Once again, God was watching over us and we arrived home safely without any further incidents.

When I returned the RV on the following Monday, I was still upset about the trouble we had experienced. I told the mechanic in precise detail about the incident we had with the windshield during the storm. I was convinced he would immediately climb into the RV and examine the problem. Instead, he merely shrugged and said that I was not the first one to complain about that issue. I was stunned the company would continue to allow customers and employees drive this vehicle without fixing the defect. In retrospect, it was the mid-seventies and quality was not a primary concern of US manufacturers.

Those who fail to learn the lessons of history are doomed to repeat them.

Based on our experience with the RV, we should have been more wary of accepting another vacation opportunity, especially one that had a vehicle associated with it. Gail's Uncle Tony and his wife had an Airstream trailer permanently parked at Chautauqua Lake in western New York. They offered us the use of the trailer for a week if we would dog sit their toy poodle, Fluffy, while they were on a trip to Arizona. The offer seemed too good to be true; watching a small dog in exchange for staying in a luxurious trailer on a lake in a very popular resort area. Unfortunately, it was! What they failed to disclose, I'm sure purely unintentional, was the dog was extremely high-strung and had a hypersensitive digestive system, a condition we discovered soon enough.

Logistics was our initial concern. How to fit seven kids, our five plus Ray, and Mary, two adults and a dog, along with a week's supply of food, clothes and diapers into one station wagon. I purchased a car top carrier to ease the burden, and most of the clothes, diapers and some food were packed into our "Big Mac," the name the kids affectionately labeled our car top carrier because it looked like a Big Mac container. To say it was crowded would be an understatement. But we didn't mind because we were going to spend a week on a lake at one of the most desired vacation locations in western New York State.

They dropped off the dog and the keys to the trailer on Friday morning on their way to the airport. We left for New York that night to optimize the amount of time we would have at the lake. Unfortunately, we didn't pay any attention to the weather forecast. It started raining about an hour into our trip and continued to pour for the next two and a half hours. In addition, the dog had diarrhea which necessitated several stops along the way in the rain to allow it to relieve itself.

By the time we arrived, it was still raining hard and Gail and I were not talking to each other. I was upset because, if we had left at the time I had planned to leave, we would have avoided most of the rain. She was upset because I was being so inconsiderate and thoughtless, not appreciating how difficult and time consuming it was to get everything ready for nine people to go on a week's vacation, starting time be damned. That's the mood we both were in when we arrived and started to unpack in the dark. Then we discovered our car top carrier was not water tight. Everything in the carrier, including the cloth diapers was soaked. Our dispositions soured even further. After unloading the station wagon into the trailer in the rain, Ray and I left, hoping to find a laundromat open at midnight in order to dry some of the clothes and diapers for the next few days. We were successful and spent the next hour or so, stuffing several empty dryers with rain soaked clothing and quarters. When we returned, the mood inside the trailer hadn't improved.

The first full day was spent sorting through the mess, replacing the food stuffs that were too wet and damaged to use and getting acclimated to the area. We even bought rope and clothes pins for a clothesline to complete the job of drying the clothes. The rain didn't stop until late afternoon so the nine of us and a sick dog became very cozy in the trailer.

The weather on Sunday was clear, sunny and warm. In spite of having a temperamental dog with digestive problems, our negative attitudes began to melt with the bright sunshine. After church, we decided to spend the day at the beach. The trailer was no more than a couple hundred yards from the edge of the lake. After a few hours of playing on the beach and in the water, everyone was ready for a break. I headed back to our home away from home to get some refreshments for the kids and adult beverages for Gail and me. I opened the door and water rushed out. I ran inside to find the carpet soaked with water. Panicking,

I looked around for the source of the leak. After checking the faucets and the toilet, I saw water coming from under a panel in the back of the vehicle. I frantically searched the trailer for a tool box which I finally found in a far corner of a closet, and was able to unscrew the panel. A hose that connected the water line to the outside source of water for the camper had ruptured and the water was pouring into the trailer. I ran outside and turned off the water at the outside source. That stopped the flow of water, but also cut off the water supply to the camper. Lying on the soaked carpet, I was able to reach under the structure and unscrew the clamps holding the damaged hose.

I returned to the beach, without any snacks or refreshments, to tell everyone what had happened. After I finished my tale of woe, Gail and I went back to the camper to try and clean up as best we could. Ray and Mary stayed with the younger kids at the beach. After removing several wet things from inside the trailer to sun dry, I left, hoping to find a hardware store open and get a new hose. Without a new hose, we had no water. When I finally found a hardware store, I carried the hose with me to make sure I got the right size replacement. Much to my chagrin, the store owner told me he did not carry that type of pressure hose. He suggested I try an auto repair shop for a possible replacement, but they were closed on Sunday. He also mentioned an RV dealership on the other side of town as a possible source, but they, too, were closed Sunday. I was disheartened as I headed back to the campgrounds.

We spent the rest of the day portaging pails of water from the public shower area for our water needs. On Monday morning after breakfast, I left for the RV dealership and the best hope for replacing the broken hose. After explaining my dilemma to the guy behind the parts counter, he lifted my spirits tremendously when he said he thought he had a replacement. He took my damaged hose and within a few minutes returned with a suitable match. I gladly paid the cost and headed out feeling like a new man. By noon we had water again.

On Tuesday, Gail and Mary took the kids to do some shopping and explore the various stores in town. Ray and I stayed behind with the suffering dog. I anticipated they would be gone for a few hours. After about five hours, I became concerned. With no other car and no means of communication, all I could do was worry and wait. When they finally returned, I could see from her demeanor, Gail was upset. She told me they lost Kristin, who had just turned three, and couldn't find her. When they discovered she was missing, they frantically retraced their steps through the stores they had visited, searching for her. After many anxious minutes, they finally found her in one of the clothing stores. The owner had discovered her unattached and kept her busy with toys until the group returned. Apparently, Kristin had either wandered away or lingered behind looking at something when the rest left. After they found her, Gail hugged Kristin tightly, and then gave her a stern lecture about wandering off on her own. As with many things in life, it often takes more than once to learn a lesson.

After an auspicious opening night in a rainstorm that rivaled Noah's, a flooded camper, and a lost child two days later, the rest of the week was relatively uneventful, except for lingering doggy difficulties. We were able to get the carpeting dry and everything in the camper back together. By Friday, we'd had our fill of camper living, despite the fine accommodations and the tourist attractions the area had to offer. So, after lunch we sent the kids to the beach for one final swim while Gail and I packed the car and cleaned the trailer one final time. When the kids finished at the beach, they showered at the outdoor facilities, changed, and we headed for home during daylight with no rain in the forecast. The ride back was uneventful. Even the dog cooperated.

In the spring of 1978, almost two years after we moved to Wisconsin, we planned to visit Gail's brother, Frank, and his family over Easter break. They were living in Mandeville, Louisiana, a suburb of New Orleans. Since we only had limited time, and couldn't afford to fly with five kids, between the ages of five to twelve, we debated between driving and taking a train. A bus was never an option. Driving meant a seventeen hour continuous trip one way, with seven of us and luggage stuffed in the limited confines of an older station wagon. Contrast that hassle with a relaxing train ride which would enhance the overall experience of the vacation and allow us to arrive well rested, refreshed and ready to go.

We opted for the train, despite the much higher cost, because it was a unique opportunity for the family *to ride the rails*. A blurb from an Amtrak brochure helped influence our decision. "Your journey on the City of New Orleans takes you through the heart of our nation's musical heritage—from Chicago with its world-class Chicago Symphony Orchestra and still vibrant electric blues scenes, to Beale Street in Memphis. Then travel the history-laden musical crossroads of Mississippi to New Orleans—the birth place of jazz. You'll be riding in the shadows of giants of American music like Louis Armstrong, Robert

Johnson, Muddy Waters and Elvis Presley." Not only were we persuaded, we felt like we should pack a trumpet or saxophone to reap the full cultural benefit of this ride. Besides, what could possibility go wrong on an Amtrak train ride from Milwaukee to The Big Easy?

Let me count the ways. First of all, we had to transfer trains at Chicago's Union Station, which meant we had to unload all our belongings from one train in the midst of busy commuter traffic and find the next train before it was scheduled to leave. Fifty minutes can go by quickly when you are trapped in an underground cavern with a multitude of people heading in every which way and we weren't sure where to go next. We wandered around, carrying or dragging our belongings, trying to keep everyone together, and looked for a sign or a railroad official who could give us some directions. Neither was readily available. Finally, a friendly traveler must have either overheard our increasingly desperate conversation or noticed our peril. She gave us very specific instructions on where to go to catch the train to New Orleans. She even accompanied us partway to make sure we headed in the right direction. We arrived with minutes to spare and climbed aboard one of the cars.

We had not anticipated how crowded the train would be. I guess we weren't the only ones who thought a train ride to New Orleans might be a fun way to spend spring break. There were scattered empty seats throughout the car, but none of them together. After checking out two other cars and finding the same crowded conditions, we ended up filling the available seats on one of the cars. No more than two of us sat side-by-side or across the aisle at any time during the trip. Since there were seven of us, one had to sit alone. I drew the short straw to begin the trip and ended up sitting next to a stranger who was not in the mood to carry on a conversation. After I tried to introduce myself and got no response, I got the message. I was glad I brought along plenty of reading material.

Because of the large number of travelers, there were always long lines for the restrooms. This proved to be problematic near the end of the trip when the toilets began to overflow, rendering them inoperable and off-limits. So much for the luxury of avoiding stopping every time someone had to use the bathroom. In addition, the offensive odor emanating from those rooms permeated the entire car.

Gail had packed plenty of food for the trip. We had pepperoni bread, sandwiches of specialty Italian lunchmeat on homemade buns, cookies, fruit snacks, chips and sodas. Our family became the envy of the car, especially when the dining service on the train ran out of food about sixteen hours into the trip. One of the passengers, jokingly, asked one of our boys to check with their mother to see if she would sell him a sandwich. When our son got out of his seat to check, the rider grabbed his arm and said he was only kidding. If we would have been true entrepreneurs, we could have easily sold the remaining supply we had and offset the cost of the tickets.

The route we traveled was less than idyllic. Unlike the brochures which describe a tranquil passage through rolling plains and abundant farmland, we saw plenty of the backsides of abandoned buildings, dilapidated industrial areas and poverty-ridden sections of our country. The old adage about being from the wrong side of the tracks took on greater meaning after that ride.

Grandpa, You Have Old Hair

It seemed like almost every vacation we took, the weather, usually rain, had an adverse impact on our getaway. In this case, it was the amount of rain that had fallen throughout the mid-south prior to our departure. Due to an unusually wet early spring, the track beds were super saturated with moisture which restricted the speed the train could travel. As a result, the projected seventeen hour trip lasted more than twenty-five hours. When we finally arrived, we were neither well-rested nor refreshed.

Before my retirement, I had been to the Wisconsin State Fair only once with our family. On that particular day, we experienced all the things the fair had to offer. We toured many barns, saw a number of different animals, watched various judgings, and listened to the spiels of the fair hucksters. After visiting the cream puff building, we headed over to a picnic area for a breather. When we counted noses, we came up one nose short. Kristin was missing! We thought she was with us in the last venue, but we weren't absolutely sure. After the initial panic of discovering we had lost one of our children, we frantically retraced our steps to try and find her among the crowds.

We searched for probably fifteen minutes, but it seemed more like two hours. Then a family friend, with Kristin on his shoulders, found us and asked, "Did we lose anything of value recently?" Somehow she got separated from the rest of the family in the cream puff pavilion and began to wander around looking for us. Fortunately, our friend saw her and asked where the rest of her family was. When she told him she was looking for them, he stayed with her until we connected.

After that harrowing experience, we decided to celebrate Kristin's return and buy a few of the creamy desserts to share.

Not exactly the large feast the father held for the return of his prodigal son, but we were on a limited budget! When cutting a cream puff, there is always excess whipped cream remaining on the wrapping paper. What better thing to do with the excess than whip it (pun intended) at your sister. Greg decided to use a plastic spoon to propel a glob of whipped cream. He loaded up the spoon, cocked it, aimed at Terri, and let it fly. It missed her, but managed to hit a man sitting with his back to us right in the bald spot! He wiped the glob from his head and turned to find out where it came from. Before he realized what happened, I ran over to the guy and apologized (for the lousy aim of my son), and offered him my hanky to clean off the rest of the mess. I half expected him to punch me in the process, but he graciously accepted my apology, got up and left.

As soon as he was outside of earshot, our kids roared with laughter. They couldn't believe Greg's audacious maneuver and were really teasing him. Greg, thinking he was in serious trouble, denied he really intended to hit Terri, but was only trying to get a reaction out of her and the spoon slipped. After that mishap, the rest of the day was rather uneventful. It was more than twenty years before I returned.

When Gail had the great idea of celebrating Steven's sixth birthday tent camping at Peninsula State Park in the middle of October, I had some misgivings because of the time of year. Maybe she was trying to justify our recent purchase of an eight man tent at a going out of business sale. We should have realized this was probably not the most desirable time of the year to camp at Peninsula when we had no trouble getting reservations on short notice for a campsite at the most popular park in Wisconsin. We didn't think, plan or pack for snow and below freezing temperatures, both of which we encountered on the first night.

We were able to find our campsite okay, but trying to pitch an eight man tent with a twenty mph wind in the blowing snow was not an easy task. Although I had practiced putting it up in our backyard, I hadn't anticipated dealing with the elements. After struggling with each step in the process, we finally got it up. Then we left for a famous Door County outdoor fish boil. Weather aside, the experience was disappointing. It was too crowded and the food was bland.

Later that night we were so cold in the tent, we had to put on several layers of clothing, including hats and gloves, to go to bed, even though we were sleeping in sleeping bags. Even that wasn't enough. When I woke up in the middle of the night, my mustache was frozen to the sleeping bag (only a slight exaggeration). I think we set a new record for the lowest temperature for that date in that part of the state.

When we opened the tent flap in the morning, we were greeted by two inches of fresh snow on the ground. It was beautiful to look at, but posed a problem trying to cook breakfast over a campfire with snow-covered, wet wood. After several attempts to get the wet wood to catch fire, I finally succeeded and got a blaze worthy of a more seasoned outdoorsman, courtesy of several editions of old newspaper rolled up tightly. I looked around for some acknowledgement from other campers in the area. We were all alone. There was no one within acres of us. The good news was we were able to gather as much fallen scrap wood as we needed to maintain the flame. After my near-heroic effort to provide heat, Gail took over the more mundane task of cooking for the three of us over a campfire: eggs, once over lightly; bacon, crispy and moist; and hash browns, slightly crunchy on the outside, but tender on the inside. Mission accomplished!

The sun did come out later in the morning, melting the snow, and we had much more favorable weather for the balance of the weekend. We did some hiking over several scenic, but soggy trails, explored a small cave on the side of a hill, and visited a late nineteenth century lighthouse. The fall colors were close to their peak, creating an inviting and vibrant backdrop to our outdoor adventure.

On Sunday afternoon the tent came down easier than it went up, especially since we did not have to contend with the lack of daylight and the unruly elements. After lowering it to the ground and taking inventory of all the pegs and poles, I stuffed the contents into the carrying bag and threw the entire package into the back seat of the car. Although Steven enjoyed the fall outdoor experience, despite the crazy weather we had on the first night, he never asked to go camping again. Also, I think he began to have some misgivings about his parents' judgment (or lack thereof), trying to spend the weekend outdoors in what seemed like the middle of winter.

No vacation chapter would be complete without at least a mention of our trip to South Dakota. Greg and Margie, our son and daughter-in-law, were living in Brookings, SD. Gail and Steven had made a previous trip to help out during Margie's pregnancy, but this time, we were going on vacation. We planned to visit Mt. Rushmore, drive through the Badlands, and stay at Custer State Park. This trip agenda could have been lifted directly from a "Visit South Dakota" vacation brochure. Our group included sons, Brian and Steven, Grandma Ray, Uncle Chuck, Greg, Margie and their six month old daughter, Frances, Gail and yours truly. The one uncontrolled variable, the chink in the armor, was the weather.

When we left Greg's house on the eastern edge of the state and headed west, it was raining hard, so hard the water was halfway up our tires in some low spots. (Reread the first quote at the beginning of this chapter.) We had a caravan of three vehicles. Over the next seven days, we experienced record-shattering rainfall, flooding conditions and soggy groceries; Uncle Chuck was almost trampled by a herd of buffalo while he crept up on a solitary, grazing bison, trying to get a close-up picture of the massive bull; getting lost (yet again) on the way to the Badlands and ending up in Wyoming; hitting an overhead awning at a motel with a bike mounted on a rack on the top of a car; being bumped in the rear of the car from someone in our traveling party while parked and waiting for another one in our party to complete nature's call; removing a tick from Steven's head; being alarmed (fortunately, a false alarm) about Grandma Ray possibly having a heart attack on the walkway leading to Mt. Rushmore; and losing money at a near record pace at one of the local casinos. All this in one week.

On a more positive note, we did experience a truly patriotic moment while visiting Mt. Rushmore at night. With spotlights dancing on the faces of the presidents and the Star Spangled Banner playing in the background, we stood with our hands over our hearts, proud to be citizens of this great country. And, of course, we stopped at Wall Drug, the most famous drugstore west of the Mississippi, after seeing what seemed like a hundred signs on the highway advertising the place.

As we were standing outside the Corn Palace in Mitchell, SD, in the rain, debating whether or not we should spend the money to see this "attraction," Steven spotted the headline of a local newspaper at a newsstand. It read, "Clinton Declares South Dakota a Disaster Area." With his tongue firmly planted in his cheek, he questioned glibly, "What took him so long?"

To infer that all our vacations were disasters would be a gross misrepresentation. We had many wonderful vacations. For almost ten years we spent five days during late July with the Foxes at their summer home on Green Lake. Their oldest five kids and our oldest five kids were of similar ages and all went to school together. We would swim, fish (some better than others), water-ski (some better than others), sail, jump in the lake from tires, go horseback riding (some better than others), cook out, PLAY BRIDGE, and enjoy each other's company. At night the kids played spoons, other card games and just did things kids do to amuse themselves while their parents played endless rubbers of bridge. Without television we all learned to have fun the old-fashioned way. It was relaxing, refreshing and rewarding.

In late July, 2010, the McMullens, Sutherlands and Noels held a family reunion in Missouri. The idea originated with Frank nearly a year earlier, and after everyone agreed it would be worth the effort to try, he conveniently turned the planning and execution (read all the work) over to Tim McMullen and Brian Noel to make it happen. After considerable coordination and research, Brian located a suitable place at the Holiday Shores Resort in Lake of the Ozarks, Missouri. It was somewhat centrally located for everyone from Minnesota, Wisconsin and Ohio to Tennessee, Georgia and Florida, could accommodate a large group (over 70), and was available in late July. Collectively, we made the commitment to go forward and put down a deposit for eight lakefront cottages. It proved to be a great decision. The cottages were right on the water and were close to each other. It was like our own compound, with people coming and going throughout the day and night. The property owner made available a large outdoor grill and expansive canopied eating area with tables and chairs for our exclusive use. Consequently, we ate all our evening meals as a group.

In addition to the obvious swimming, fishing and various watercrafts, we golfed, hiked, tossed water balloons in towels, and played soccer during the day, and plenty of cards and other games at night. The different families blended well and the cousins developed new friendships with their relatives.

The only downside to the week was the hot, hot weather. It reached the upper nineties during most of the days we were there. Everyone agreed that the reunion was a stunning success and we should try to do it again in two years. That was eight years ago!

Gail and I have been to Mexico twice. The first time, in 2004, we stayed at a beautiful resort in Cabo San Lucas. Aside from the near ear-splitting din that greeted us outside the airport where every vendor within a five mile radius was screaming at the top of their lungs trying to sell us something, the trip was peaceful and relaxing. The weather was ideal and we had no schedule to follow. Wonderful accommodations, margaritas at the infinity pool in the afternoon, leisurely late night dinners at one of the three restaurants on site, and no morning wake-up calls.

Because we had rented a car, we were able to leave the property and explore the surrounding area. One day we drove to San Jose Del Cabo, another resort town, approximately 20 miles from Cabo San Lucas, where we experienced firsthand a holiday celebration of Dia de Muertos, the Day of the Dead. Local families met on the plaza and set up small altars on the walkways decorated with candles, drawings and pictures commemorating the lives of their departed relatives. Some individuals were even in native dress and celebrated with music and dance.

Another evening we drove to the tip of the Baja California peninsula and took an evening dinner cruise which started on the Sea of Cortez and traveled to where the water merged with the Pacific Ocean. We dined with two couples from Canada and spent a wonderful evening enjoying each other's company. After meeting them for a nightcap at their hotel, we walked back to the parking lot to retrieve our rented car. Unfortunately, I forgot where I had parked and there were three separate lots from which to choose. We spent almost an hour looking for the car. A small price to pay for such a wonderful evening.

Two years later, shortly after the birth of their second child, our son, Brian, and his wife proposed we take a family vacation trip with both sets of parents to Oaxaca, Mexico. It was intended to be a *thank you* for helping out during and after Rosa's second pregnancy. Although Rosa's parents grew up in Mexico, neither had been to Oaxaca. It is a unique area in southern Mexico, known for its indigenous history and customs, historic ruins, many fine restaurants, featuring local cuisine, and beautiful churches and cathedrals. Based on our experience in Cabo, Gail and I were all in. The adults began planning early for a fall getaway. This was going to be a memorable trip, one we would long remember.

There was one small problem. In the fall, 2006, Oaxaca was experiencing considerable civil unrest. Rioting occurred sporadically throughout the city. It started earlier in the year when the police fired on a group of striking teachers who were trying to take over a city administration building. As a result of that action, the protests grew in intensity and frequency. This may have been the right place, but it was definitely the wrong time. By the time we found out about these problems, we had already purchased our plane tickets and paid a sizable down payment on a local residence where we planned to stay. We were reluctant to walk away from our financial investment without any return. When we contacted the airline about a possible refund if we didn't make the trip because of the turmoil, they were unwilling to reimburse us for the tickets without an advisory from the State Department cautioning Americans not travel to this part of Mexico.

We carefully monitored State Department bulletins regarding the dangers involved in U.S. citizens traveling to Oaxaca, *little to no risk for Americans*, and closely followed online chatrooms of people who had recently visited that part of Mexico, *wonderful trip with no concerns or disruptions*. We convinced ourselves the trip was safe. Since no tourists had been harmed during the political upheaval, we decided to go. We landed at Oaxaca's airport on a Friday afternoon after a lengthy 15 hour trip with a stop in Houston to change planes. We planned to stay for ten days.

Brian and Rosa's kids, Samuel, age two, and Gabriella, a day shy of her first birthday, handled the long flight extremely well, much better than their parents and grandparents. They slept when they were supposed to sleep and played, with the help of both Grandmas, for much of the remainder of the time. Since Rosa and her parents were fluent in Spanish, we navigated the airport obstacles and Mexican customs without any major delays or mishaps. After collecting our luggage, we hired a driver to take us to our new temporary residence.

Our trip from the airport to the house was eye-opening. There was very little traffic, but we saw several cars and small pickup trucks overturned on the side of the road. Many buildings, including churches, were spray-painted with slogans and signs. At one intersection, there was an abandoned school bus with smashed windows and graffiti all over its side. According to our driver, anarchists had taken over the leadership of the teachers' union during the summer and were successful in forcing the police out of the central part of the city, a fun fact we were unaware of until that drive. Our driver tried to minimize the danger and devastation, but, to us, it looked like a scene in a war zone. We seriously questioned our decision to make the trip.

When we arrived at the address we had given the driver, we saw nothing but a high concrete wall surrounding the property. Anxiety and uncertainty overcame the adults as we waited silently in the parked vehicle to see what was behind the wall. Our driver jumped out and knocked on a wooden door embedded in the structure. A woman opened the door slightly and spoke to the driver. After a brief conversation, she swung the door open and invited us into the house. We stumbled out of the vehicle while the driver unloaded the luggage. After settling our fare, we walked apprehensively into the home through an inner door and gazed around at our new surroundings.

Our hostess introduced herself as Francisca Gutierrez in flawless English and welcomed us to the property. After securing the luggage and giving Samuel and Gabriella a special welcoming pat on the cheek, she led us on a tour of the house. On the first floor surrounding one side of a large open courtyard of slate tile and colored stone cut outs was a huge, well-equipped, modern kitchen and a dining area furnished with a heavy rustic table and matching chairs. On one of the kitchen counters was a selection of pastries for us.

Toward the front of the house was a comfortable sitting room with several chairs, end tables and couches. One part of an inside wall contained several shelves of books. Most of the titles were in Spanish, but there was one section with English selections. On the opposite side of the courtyard was a large bedroom, big enough for a queen-size bed and two overstuffed chairs. On the second floor, accessible via a winding staircase, were four more good-sized bedrooms. The house was neat, clean and tastefully decorated; a welcome refuge from the chaos outside its walls.

As we were walking through the house, Francisca explained that she and her husband had purchased this residence more than a year ago as an investment property and planned to rent it out to tourists visiting the area. Initially, she said, they were successful and it was occupied most of the time. With all the turmoil going on in the city over the last few months, the rentals dried up and she and her husband had been taking turns staying at the house to protect their investment from break-ins and damage. She thanked us repeatedly for choosing to stay at their place.

Despite the local unrest, we did manage to do some

sightseeing, walking around the town and visiting some of the local churches. Unfortunately, even the historic cathedral in the center of the square with beautiful stained glass windows had not escaped the spray can of the graffiti vandals.

One morning we hired a driver and ventured out a few hours from our residence to visit Monte Alba, a top tourist attraction in the area according to a one of the travel guides. It was an archeological site of an ancient Zapotec seat of power. On the way back we stopped and took a tour of a small distillery producing mescal from cactus leaves the old-fashioned way. Of course, they had samples, adults only, and products to sell.

Blas, Rosa's dad, was usually the first one up in the morning and he would go to the mercado to purchase food and other provisions for the day and listen in on some of the local gossip. On Wednesday, he returned to the house very upset. He had overheard a few of the vendors talking about a possible full-scale riot in town on Friday with the intent of occupying the mayor's headquarters and removing him from office. Because there were no police, the state militia had been put on alert.

A few of the merchants Blas had become acquainted with during our visit urged him to get his family out of the area before the rioting started. Because Blas considered our safety his responsibility, he was insistent that we leave immediately. We checked with the airline to see if we could change our tickets from Sunday to Thursday. Even though they had seats available, they were unwilling to make any accommodation without charging a hefty price for the change. They kept insisting there was no emergency evacuation. After a brief discussion of the pros and cons of staying until Sunday, we reluctantly agreed to pay the additional cost and booked reservations for the Thursday flight. We notified Francisca we would be leaving early, but insisted she keep the full rental. It was the least we could do to thank her for the gracious hospitality and accommodations she had provided us.

As we boarded the plane on Thursday, we all agreed on one thing. This was a trip we would long remember.

Chapter 5: Vehicles in Our Lives

"I want my own pit crew…I hate the procedure I currently have to go through when I have car problems." – Dave Berry

"Is fuel efficiency really what we need most desperately? I say what we really need is a car that can be shot when it breaks down." – Russell Baker

You already read about the rented cement truck without brakes and the car with the damaged back door that didn't close properly. Those were only a few links in a chain of vehicles we have connected with throughout the years. During my college days, I had very little money and less mechanical ability. (I really haven't improved much in either category.) When I attended John Carroll University, I lived at home and drove to school every day. I would buy cars for less than $100, which usually meant they were more than ten years old, and drive them until they had a major issue (a car problem, as well as beauty, is in the eye of the beholder). Then I would junk that car, get $25 for the scrap value, and invest that money in another clunker. During those years, I owned a 1950 Pontiac (affectionately known as The Tank) with a leaky master brake cylinder which required adding brake fluid almost as often a filling up with gas, a 1951 Dodge that had a rusted out floor on the passenger's side—which the floor mat only partially covered—and a 1953 red Ford convertible with a white top.

I was driving the Dodge to class one morning to turn in a term paper which was sitting loose on a book on the passenger's side front seat. (Why it was not in a binder, paper clipped or stapled, I don't remember. I guess it wouldn't have made as good a story if it was.) This was a paper Gail had stayed up typing almost the entire night prior so I could turn it in on time. I was rushing to make the start of the class, which was not unusual during those days, and had to slam on the brakes to avoid something up ahead. The book flopped on the floor and individual pages began spilling through the large hole in the floorboard. I stopped the car, jumped out and began chasing down the street to retrieve several pages of the paper. I was able to retrieve all the pages and reassemble them in the correct order, but arrived a little later than usual. Can you imagine the comment I would have received from the professor if I told him I was late because I lost part of my paper through a hole in my car?

The prize of the collection was the 1953 red Ford convertible with a white top (emphasis on convertible) that had been in at least one accident before I got it. I bought it from a friend for $75, knowing it had seen better days. It had a bad front end, a faulty ignition switch, a front passenger door that wouldn't open (maybe *two* accidents), and a defective hood latch that once released and lifted straight up when I was driving. I couldn't see anything but a wall of red paint about a foot in front of me. After screaming a few obscenities, I was able to pull off to the side of the road by using the inside mirror and the one side mirror that wasn't broken. I got out, lowered the hood as far as it would go, climbed up on the front of the car and literally jumped on top of the hood to force it down the rest of the way. Then I casually walked back into the car and continued my journey.

The worst incident with that car occurred when Gail and I were driving on the freeway, doing about sixty-five, when the front passenger tire blew out. That was a scary scene. Despite the traffic, I was able to maneuver the car to the inside shoulder and change the tire while the cars continued to whiz past us. I think I junked that car the next day.

I didn't know owning or renting bad vehicles was genetic, but after thinking about this section, I'm not sure. Our son, Gary, was the central character in most of the rest of the vehicle incidents. (Could there be a genetic connection through the *name*?) After graduating from Northwestern and accepting a job at Inland Steel in northern Indiana, he rented a "small" twenty-six foot van to move his belongings from school to his new apartment. For the uninitiated, a van that size is large enough to move a seven room house full of furniture and belongings and still have room to move an outside children's swing set and playground accessories. Gary had enough furniture and personal belongs to fill maybe 10% of the truck, but he was also picking up a weight set for a friend who was living in Indiana. He must have wanted to make sure he had enough space. With the amount of room available, he could have transported an entire college weight room. To justify his rationale for the large truck, he tried to tell us it was the only one available.

After loading the van with his stuff, he proceeded to drive the truck on Lake Shore Drive through the city of Chicago, narrowly missing several overhanging power lines. We found out later a truck that size was not permitted on that section of Lake Shore Drive because of the potential traffic hazard it would cause if one of those wires caught on the top of the truck and snapped. Deep down I think Gary was getting even with the police for arresting him and putting him in jail (literally locking him up) when he was in college for making an illegal left hand turn on Dempster Avenue during the morning rush hour. Can you imagine the look on his fellow inmates when he answered the question why he was in jail?

Shortly after starting to work at Inland Steel after college, Gary began looking for a beater truck he could drive back and forth to the mill. (What guy doesn't want a truck?) He found an old stick shift, Chevy pickup truck in Waukesha that had some brake issues, i.e. metal to metal squeal when you pressed the brake pedal. When I saw it, I had flashbacks to the cars I drove in college. He bought the truck despite contrary advice from his dad.

Now he needed to get the truck to Indiana. Since he wanted his car there as well, I ended up driving the truck from Waukesha to his apartment in Indiana. That wasn't much of a problem except for every time I had to stop the truck. Do you have any idea how many traffic lights and toll booths (pre-I-Pass) are between Waukesha, Wisconsin and Crown Point, Indiana? More than a few! I still have nightmares about those squealing brakes.

Gail, Brian and Steven followed at a safe distance in our car. After finally arriving in Indiana, shaken but still in one piece, I parked in the lot in front of his apartment. Gary greeted us and promised me he would get the brakes fixed at the first opportunity he had. Apparently, Indiana is not the land of opportunity, because when he sold the truck a year and a half later, the brakes were in the same miserable condition they were when they first arrived.

The next vehicle incident also involved Gary, and again, featured a move. He, Kris and their four kids were living in an apartment in St. Paul, MN for too many months while waiting for their new house to be built in White Bear Lake. The day finally arrived for them to move into their beautiful new home. They couldn't get out of that apartment fast enough.

Gary made arrangements to rent a truck for Saturday morning. Gail and I drove up from Wisconsin the night before so we could help them pack and move out of the apartment. This time the truck was sized correctly, the brakes worked, but the clutch didn't. For those who have never driven a stick shift vehicle, the clutch is necessary to change gears. Consequently, the truck had only one forward gear and no reverse. The person at the rental agency apologized for the condition of the truck, but claimed that was the only one he had available. It must have been a big truck rental weekend in St. Paul.

Since there was no other option, we took that truck and made several trips to move all the furniture. Remember, we couldn't back up, so we had to maneuver the truck across several parking places in the apartment parking lot to load it. More than a few of the residents had harsh words towards us for taking up so many parking spaces. We didn't have the time or the patience to explain to each of them the problem with the truck. At the other end, we had to park in the street and carry everything up the drive and into the house because we couldn't back the truck up. Somehow, we completed the move without a major incident.

Grandpa, You Have Old Hair

When Gary returned the truck, the manager of the truck rental outlet had the audacity to ask if everything went well with the truck. My son glared at him, and then decided it wasn't worth it to tell him what he could do with his truck.

One final story about vehicles and it doesn't involve Gary. Gail's brother, Ray, purchased a new car and asked if one of our kids would like his old Honda. It had almost two hundred thousand miles on it, but it was still a serviceable vehicle for local driving. The one condition was we had to drive it from Minnesota to Wisconsin.

Gail, Brian, Steven and I made the initial trip to Minnesota. Gail and Steven planned to stay in Minnesota for two weeks to babysit Ray and Ang's four children while they were on a vacation trip. Since I didn't have a lot of vacation, I planned to drive home and return in two weeks to retrieve them.

Because I was driving a company car which no one else in the family was supposed to drive because of insurance, Brian came along as the designated driver to drive Ray's old car back to Wisconsin. There was only one glitch. The car had a manual transmission and Brian had never driven a stick shift. I gave him a two day crash course (figuratively, not literally) around the neighborhood. By Saturday night, he had almost eliminated grinding gears as he shifted, lurching forward in herky-jerky motions, and stalling out after he came to a stop.

We headed back to Wisconsin on a Sunday afternoon and planned to make only one stop on the way to minimize the number of times Brian had to go through the process of changing gears. Sometimes, life has a way of altering plans. The weather was crummy, rainy with strong winds. Traffic was unusually heavy on the interstate that afternoon, even stop and go in some spots. Driving the Honda, Brian had to change speeds frequently, which meant he had to shift gears often. He battled through as best he could, despite the sweaty arm pits down to his waist. He didn't stall once on the freeway. By the time we reached Waukesha, Brian was almost proficient in driving stick and had expanded his vocabulary by more than a few expletives.

Chapter 6: Miscellany

"Some speak in such exaggerations and superlatives that we need to make a large discount from their statements before we can come at their real meaning." – Tryon Edwards

"The words you speak today should be soft and tender, for tomorrow you may have to eat them." – Anonymous

There are many other incidents that need to be included in this brief history, but don't conveniently fall into a particular category. For instance, when our three older kids were in high school together, the morning routine was as precise as a two-minute drill in football. Since we had only one bathroom upstairs, timing was critical. I was the first one in the bathroom. While I was in the shower, Gary and Greg would use the bathroom. As soon as the three of us finished, Terri would take her turn. All of us would then dress, eat breakfast and leave together for school/work. There was no time to waste. I dropped them off at Catholic Memorial and then proceeded to work. Everything had to be synchronized without a wasted minute in order for all of us to be on time.

One morning, I was in the shower and Gary was at the sink. I reached for the shampoo on the ledge of the tub, lost my footing, fell against the shower curtain, and tumbled out of the shower. To cover for my embarrassment and clumsiness, I quickly got up and jumped back into the shower without saying a word. There was no time for an explanation because I didn't want to be the one to make us late. Gary looked, but never said anything. At breakfast there was normally not a lot of conversation, so nothing was said about the incident. I could only imagine what Gary thought during the rest of the day about his dad doing a tumbling routine in and out of the shower to start the day.

At dinner that night Gary regaled for the rest of the family the happenings of the morning. When he got to the part about me standing up and jumping back into the shower without saying a word, he could no longer contain himself and burst into uncontrollable laughter. He must have been holding it in all day and finally had the opportunity to release the emotion. I sat there stone-faced and mortified. Gail leaned over and asked me why I didn't say something, anything, like "I'm fine," or I'm okay." My only defense was there wasn't a lot to say and I didn't want to waste time making excuses. We all had a good laugh over the unusual balancing act of that morning.

If you've read the previous sections, you must have noticed there are certain recurring themes throughout the narrative. One of them is a lost child. For whatever reason, we kept losing Kristin. On this occasion, all seven of us (pre-Steven), went to a night Lenten service at St. Mary's Church. Kristin was about six at the time. After the service the kids ran down the back flight of stairs to the parking lot, and were in the car before us. Often, one or more of them would hide in the way back of the station wagon under a blanket and pretend they were not in the car.

Neither Gail nor I bothered to count noses before we left the parking lot. As soon as we reached home, the phone rang. It was a priest who had conducted the Lenten service, asking if we were missing anything or anyone. When we checked the kids, we found we didn't have Kristin. I rushed back to St. Mary's to get her, debating with myself how I was going to explain leaving her at Church. When I arrived, Father was waiting with Kristin. As soon as I started my explanation about what had happened, he stopped me and said, "No need for an explanation. These things happen in large families. But remember, in the future, when someone talks about giving up something for Lent, they're not referring to children." Then he bade us good night, turned and walked away.

I don't know who was more embarrassed over this incident, Kristin for wandering away and having to wait with Father for one of her parents to come back and pick her up, or her parents for not noticing she was missing.

We replaced our carpeting in our former home on Green Valley during a very hot August. Just ask Brian, who was participating in two-a-day football practice at the time, how hot it was that month. In order to expedite the process (and save a few bucks), we removed the old carpet ourselves. We rolled it up and temporarily stored it in our garage until we could take it to the dump. Because it was so warm outside, we kept the garage open most evenings. While the roll of carpet was still in the garage, we had an uninvited guest, an opossum, wander into the garage and set up housekeeping in the carpet. It must have liked the color of the old rug.

Greg volunteered to remove the critter. He went into the

garage, stomped his feet, clapped his hands and yelled at the animal. When the opossum made some nasty sounds and bared its teeth at Greg's initial overture, Greg decided to get serious. He went in the house and put on his catcher's equipment: shin guards, chest protector and mask, and grabbed a bat. He was prepared to do battle. When the opossum saw Greg decked out in full armor, it must have decided discretion was the better part of valor, and slowly vacated the premises. Wouldn't you like to know the story that 'possum told his buddies that night about his encounter with the baseball knight?

Grandpa Calabrese, Gail's grandfather, had several old-country sayings that he brought with him from Italy. One of his favorites was, "Laugh today, cry tomorrow." That old adage was quite apropos to the events that occurred within our family in a one week span mid-October, 1985. On October 14th, Steven was born. We were jubilant with our new baby boy. The birth was normal, and Mom and baby were healthy and fine. They came home on Thursday, and those of us at home celebrated the homecoming. Gary was at Northwestern and Greg was at Madison. Both came home on Friday to meet their new brother. That night, Greg captivated us with a hilarious story about his first exposure to a beer party at Madison. Terri laughed so hard she actually fell off a bench.

On Saturday morning Terri was up early and left to pick up three teammates for an 8:00 a.m. soccer game. The rest of us had planned to sleep in after a late night and then have a leisurely breakfast. Our calm was shattered with a phone call from the police. Terri had a serious car accident on the way to the game. They told us she was rushed from the accident scene by ambulance to Waukesha Memorial Hospital, but could not tell us any more about her condition.

Even though Gail just had a baby five days before, she insisted on going with me. We quickly dressed and rushed to the hospital, dreading what we were about to experience. Even though the hospital was only about fifteen minutes away, it seemed like an eternity. When we arrived, we found our daughter in the intensive care unit with several internal injuries. The joy and happiness from the night before changed to apprehension and anguish when we saw our oldest daughter, a senior in high school, unconscious and being closely monitored in the ICU. She had a punctured lung, several broken ribs, internal bleeding and possible head injuries. We couldn't do anything but watch and pray as she lay motionless in the bed.

Later that morning, Gail went home to nurse the baby, but returned in an hour or so. She repeated that pattern two more times that first day. In order to ease everyone's concern about wanting to be at the hospital all the time, we set up a schedule for the family so at least one member would maintain the hospital vigil until we knew more about Terri's condition. Gail still blames some of Steven's many digestive problems on nursing him during such a traumatic period.

On that first morning at the hospital, one of the other girls in the car told me what she recalled of the accident. Terri was driving my Toyota and was following a friend in a car ahead of her. She turned left onto highway 18, apparently without looking for oncoming traffic, directly in front of a car doing about fifty. She was hit on the driver's side and that part of the car collapsed in on her. The impact was so severe, the car was totaled. When

I saw the car later at the junk yard, I almost threw up knowing our daughter had been driving that car. The driver side door was pushed half way into the car and the driver's bucket seat was twisted at a forty-five degree angle. Fortunately, all four girls in the car were wearing seatbelts. The other girls were emotionally shaken, but incurred no physical injuries.

On Sunday Terri had emergency surgery to remove her damaged spleen in order to stop the internal bleeding. Initially, the doctors were hoping the spleen would heal itself, but she was losing too much blood, so they had to remove the organ. After a successful surgery and post-op recuperation, she was finally assigned to a regular room in the hospital. Ten days later, she came home to continue her convalescence. Since she didn't go back to school for another six weeks, per doctor's recommendation, Terri had plenty of time to bond with her new baby brother. As she lay on her back on the couch in the family room, Gail would gently place baby Steven on her chest so she could hold him. She would wrap her arms around the baby, tickle his cheek and make funny baby sounds to him. The two of them spent many hours in such an embrace.

While attending UW-Madison, Brian began playing team handball, a sport similar to water polo, without the water. After playing for two years at a college club level, and participating in a number of tournaments throughout the Midwest, he must have impressed someone. He, along with approximately forty other team handball athletes throughout the country, was invited to participate in a four team round robin team handball tournament at the Olympic Festival.

Started in 1978, the Olympic Festival was a US amateur

multi-sport competition, sponsored by the US Olympic Committee, and held in years between the Olympic Games. The event was designed to be the culmination of the summer training program for prospective Olympic athletes and part of the process for selecting US participants for the next Olympic Games. At the time it was the nation's largest amateur sporting event, before ending in 1995. In 1993, the Festival was held in San Antonio.

Before participating in the competition in August, Brian went to the Olympic training center in Colorado Springs for two weeks of rigorous workouts with the others selected for the team handball tryout. Since Brian was relatively new to the sport, it was quite an honor to be included with that group.

Gary and I decided to go to San Antonio for the Festival and be Brian's "posse," leaving Gail and Kris home to finish planting grass for our newly built home. Although Brian had some team activities during the day and stayed at the Olympic Festival Village, off-limits to visitors, he did have some free time. On the second day of the festival, we met him for lunch at a downtown restaurant between the morning and afternoon games. He became enamored with the macadamia nut chocolate chip cookie dessert and had to have some to take back with him to the Village. Our waitress told him the kitchen crew had run out of cookies, but were preparing another batch. He decided to wait, even though he knew he was risking being late for the pregame coach's talk. He felt he had enough time to make it back. Somehow, the cookies took longer than the server had predicted, so Brian grabbed the bag of cookies as soon as server brought them to the table, gave us a quick good-bye, and ran out of the restaurant.

He later told us he ran all the way back to the fieldhouse. It was ninety-eight degrees outside in San Antonio that afternoon. When he arrived, pouring sweat and completely out of breath, the coach was waiting for him outside the locker room. He told Brian he was scheduled to start that afternoon and then proceeded to chew him out royally for his tardiness and not being ready to play. After apologizing to his coach for his late arrival, Brian got taped up quickly, and he did start the game. He even managed to score the first goal for his team. When his substitute was sent in midway in the contest, I could see from across the court the sheepish grin he had on his face when he sat on the bench.

I'm still not sure what he did with the extra cookies he had to have before leaving the restaurant, but I don't think he offered any to his coach.

Steven's high school senior after-prom party is one of those "you're not going to believe this" kind of event. Gail and I agreed to host an after-prom party for Steve and several of his friends under certain conditions. All drivers had to surrender their keys when they arrived, no sneaking out to the cars "to get something they forgot," no alcohol, and no one could leave until after breakfast. We were not naïve enough to think there wouldn't be drinking, but with periodic adult oversight and control of the keys, at least we could confine the activity to our home and prevent it from spilling out onto the streets.

The six couples began arriving after midnight. All of them had already changed out of their formal prom attire into more comfortable clothes. We greeted them at the door and shepherded them to the basement. Since we knew most of them and their families from various high school sporting events, social activities and get-togethers over the previous four years, we weren't expecting any problems.

The noise from loud music and partying of twelve older teenagers lasted until about four. Then things quieted down. We made a final check around that time to make sure everyone had a place to sleep and enough blankets and pillows to get some rest. Since a few of the kids had jobs and other responsibilities to attend to in the morning, we scheduled breakfast for the early shift around 8:30 a.m. Gail and I cleaned up a bit and made sure everyone was bedded down before we headed to bed shortly before five.

We had been asleep for less than an hour when Steve knocked on our bedroom door and said there was water in the basement. After I finally came to, my initial thought was that the toilet had overflowed and water was running from the bathroom. When I got downstairs and my first step squished on the carpet, I realized it was far more serious than an overflowing toilet. The entire carpeted area was saturated and there was water on both sides of the basement. Looking around, I saw water pouring down the walls beneath the window wells. When I checked the sump pump, water was flowing out of the crock. The pump had failed to activate. After more than three days of continuious rain, the buildup of water around the house created pressure and flowed into the window wells. We later found out the drains in the bottom of the window wells were blocked with leaves and various other debris, so the water filled the openings and leaked through the window frames and into the basement.

The people on the floor in sleeping bags were the first to

feel the water. By the time I arrived, almost everyone was awake. Some were sitting on couches, wrapped in blankets with a dazed look of helplessness on their faces. Others were trying to rescue shoes, purses, and other paraphernalia from the water. Two wet sleeping bags were already draped over chairs and dripping onto the floor. A few of the more enterprising guests were searching for the possible cause of the problem.

I immediately grabbed a stack of towels and began putting them on the floor to absorb some water. Then we set up a conga line to transfer the wet towels to the stationery tubs on the other side of the basement, squeeze the water out, and return them to the floor to absorb more moisture. While that was going on, I ran to the garage, grabbed the shop vac and brought it downstairs. After some instructions, I assigned two boys the task of sucking up water from the carpet as quickly as they could. Finally, I went into the back room and manually worked the sump pump for more than an hour to divert the flow of water, relieve the pressure on the outside of the foundation and force the water away from the house.

Fortunately, we caught the problem early enough (thanks to the teens sleeping on the floor), to prevent any real damage to the basement. Although there was approximately an inch of water throughout the area, we were able to restore the downstairs to reasonably dry condition after a couple of days of cleanup and two dehumidifiers running full time for a week,

Not having any time to cook the planned breakfast because of the unscheduled water festivities, we sent the kids home with a sweet roll and milk or coffee. Even though they left wet, tired and hungry, they did leave with a story to tell for the rest of their lives.

Grandpa, You Have Old Hair

Our daughter, Kristin, met her husband, Dan, while both worked at Kimberly Clark. Kristin was in the engineering department at the headquarters in Neenah, and Dan was at their facility in Arkansas. Part of Kristin's job was to travel to various plants within the company to review production processes. Dan was an engineer at the Arkansas plant. They met there and began dating, despite the distance between their locations.

We first met Dan over a July Fourth holiday. Kristin, who was living in Appleton, came home for the holiday weekend. Dan, who was from Madison and whose parents still lived there, did the same. They planned to go to Summerfest together. Dan pulled into our drive in a bright red Jeep with the top off. On the back of the vehicle was a large wheel cover with Killian Red spelled out in broad letters. I winced at the graphics. To be a beer fancier was one thing, to display your preferences so boldly was worse than vanity plates.

When Kristin introduced Dan to Gail and me, she only used his first name. After a brief conversation, they headed off to Summerfest. Later that night we received a call from our daughter saying they would be home later than they planned because Dan lost his keys.

She tried to explain, "His keys must have fallen on the beach when he changed his pants, and we're still looking for them."

Suppressing my urge to question why he was changing pants on the beach, I could only think of the old adage, "You don't get a second chance to make a good first impression."

We were already in bed when Dan dropped Kristin off and headed back to Madison. The following morning Kristin tried to shed some light on the mystery of the missing keys. They were with a group at the lakefront sharing a blanket for the fireworks. As the temperature fell, Dan decided to put on jeans which were in his backpack. His keys were in his shorts pocket and they must have dropped out when he slipped them off. Since there was so much noise, nobody heard them hit the blanket.

With so many people jostling and anxious to leave after the fireworks ended, Dan didn't realize he didn't have his keys until they were well on their way to the Jeep. The group they were with immediately retraced their steps. Fortunately, they knew approximately where they had been on the beach and, after a lengthy search, found the keys.

That evening Kristin returned to her apartment in Appleton. Two days later at dinner Brian, who had met Dan and Kristin at Summerfest and was one of the group who had helped look for the keys, gave us some additional details on the events leading up to the lost keys. During the explanation, he used Dan's last name. That's how I found out his last name was Killian.

After Kristin and Dan were married, they both worked at a Kimberly Clark plant in South Carolina and lived in South Augusta, SC, just over the state line from Augusta, Georgia. Steven, Gail and I visited them over spring break in 1998. Since neither of them had a lot of vacation, the five of us spent the weekends together sightseeing and traveling around the area, but we were on our own during the week.

Since we were visiting the week after the Masters Golf tournament which is always held at the exclusive Augusta National Country Club, Steve and I drove over to the course on Tuesday morning to get a glimpse of how the other half lived. We hoped to get a tour and possibly peek into the clubhouse.

When we arrived at the front entrance, we were stopped by a security guard. He slid open his window, leaned out of the small security building, and asked if he could be of some assistance. I told him we were interested in a possible tour.

He informed me in a haughty manner, "They do not conduct tours at Augusta. The members cherish their privacy."

I then pleaded with him in my most engaging voice that my son and I were from Wisconsin and asked if we could just drive up to the clubhouse and look around. I assured him we would not disturb anyone and would not enter any building. I also threw in that my father was an avid golfer and I'd grown up watching the Masters on television.

He stared at me as if I was from a different planet and didn't understand the King's English, albeit with a distinctive southern drawl. He stepped out of the security building and I noticed he had a holster on his hip. He placed both hands on the roof of the car door and leaned through the open window. I could see blood vessels slowly expand at his temple.

He spoke very slowly, "Sir, I told you the members do not want any outsiders on the grounds." Then pointing to a small road to the right of the guard shack, he directed me in a drill sergeant's tone, "Now, turn around and go back to where you came from. I would appreciate it." He almost choked on those last four words.

I looked where he commanded me to turn around. There was a small turn around area and then the road continued toward the course. Something came over me. Maybe it was the condescending way he spoke to us. When he turned his back to return to the security post, I decided to start down the road and see what the guard would do. I left my window open so I could hear him, and kept looking in the rear view mirror as I proceeded slowly down the path. Almost immediately he jumped back out of the security station and screamed, "Turn around or I'll call the police."

I was prepared to call his bluff until he reached down and unfastened his holster. I stopped immediately and promptly began to back up. Just before reaching his station, I hit the brakes, spun the car around and didn't give him an opportunity to make another comment. I waved and drove off into the sunset (actually, it was early afternoon).

If you ever hear someone say that Augusta National is one of the most exclusive country clubs in the nation, believe him.

Chapter 7: Medical Issues

"An archaeologist is the best husband any woman can have; the older she gets, the more interested he is in her." – Agatha Christie

"Old age is not so bad when you consider the alternative." – Maurice Chevalier

I would be less than candid to write a life story about a couple growing old together and not include a section about medical issues. Have you ever listened in on conversations among elderly people, pardon me, seniors, (although some of them appear to be well on their way to graduate-level status)? It's like overhearing a high stakes poker game.

"I'll see your colonoscopy and raise you an ultrasound."
"I'll see your ultrasound and raise you a pacemaker."
"I'll see your pacemaker and raise you a knee replacement."
"I'll call because I've had all the above."

In retrospect, it is observing a game, The Game of Life.

Replacement parts are a boon to the baby boomer generation, and have been rather lucrative for the medical profession, as well. Shoulders, hips, knees and ankles—alone or in matched sets—are designed to improve mobility, reduce pain, and provide a steady income stream for the docs, therapists, and pharmacists.

Recently I went through a series of tests because I had an incident of arterial fibrillation (afib). When I completed the tests, I met with a cardiologist to discuss my medical situation. As a follow-up to the other testing I had undergone, he wanted me to do a sleep study. I resisted. Who wants to participate in a test that, if you fail, you get to sleep in a Darth Vader helmet for the rest of your life? After the doctor overwhelmed me with studies and statistics showing me why it was important to determine if sleep apnea was a possible cause for the a-fib, I reluctantly yielded to the medical version of a full court press.

When I finally agreed to the stupid thing, I had to schedule a consult with a sleep study doctor before I could proceed with the study. The earliest I could get an appointment was in three weeks. So much for the immediacy of the test. After the consult, the doctor determined I was a suitable candidate to proceed. In layman's terms, I could walk and chew gum at the same time.

I made the appropriate arrangements. On the designated day, I reported to the sleep study floor of the hospital at 8:00 p.m., favorite pillow under arm and teddy bear in hand. The technician greeted me and escorted me to the cell, aka the sleep study room. It had a bed, a chair, a lamp next to the chair and a wall-mounted television. There was a small adjacent bathroom with a toilet and sink. No windows, but no bars on the door. Next to the bed was an electronic device, about the size of a carry-on suitcase, with hundreds of wires, (well, maybe that's a slight exaggeration) plugged into it. After completing all the preliminary information, no longer called paperwork because it's all done on computer, she invited me to relax and get ready for bed. She said she would be back before ten to "hook me up."

Before leaving, she must have noticed me fixating on the torture machine next to the bed because she assured me it was nothing more than a monitor, used to record data throughout the night.

When she returned around ten, she said it was time. I felt like she was asking if I had any last minute requests before she proceeded to electrocute me. I crawled into bed and propped my teddy on a pillow next to me so he could witness every move she made. She carefully began attaching the color-coded wires to various parts of my body: ankles, calves, thighs, stomach, chest, back, neck, face, temples, and forehead. Before attaching the wires, she spread a little lubricant on each spot to help hold the patch in place and improve conductivity. When she was finished, I felt I was going to slide right out of bed. The only thing holding me in place was the hundred wires she had attached to my body.

When she finished, I asked her if she thought I was going to sleep for one minute with all the junk attached to my body. She consoled me by saying that some people didn't, but then they had to repeat the test.

I normally sleep on my stomach, but that was not permitted for the study. So I found myself lying on my back, in a strange bed, with wires attached all over my body, trying to get comfortable so I could go to sleep. Somehow I succeeded, but a short time later, the guard turned a light on and woke me up. I started to think this was all a bad dream. She told me one of the wires had come undone. She reattached the errant critter, turned off the light and wished me sweet dreams. Although I couldn't see, I swear she had a smirk on her face. Somehow I willed myself back to sleep. We repeated that exercise one more time during the night.

At six the next morning her voice came over the monitor in the room. It was time to get up, the study was over. She would be in to remove the wires. She appeared shortly, wished me a good morning, and detached the wires. That was it. I was free to get cleaned up, change and leave whenever I was ready. When I asked her about the results, she said I would be hearing from the sleep study doctor in about a week.

A week went by with no news. I began to worry. I even checked the number of electrical outlets in our bedroom to see if we had enough to accommodate the addition of the Star Wars device. Then the call came. I passed! I wouldn't have to wear a mask to go to sleep. But we were no closer to what caused the a-fib, except, "You know you're getting on in years." I didn't have to take a test to know that.

Chapter 8: Grandkids

"Grandkids are the rewards you get for not killing your kids."
– Someone far wiser than I

"Grandchildren are so much fun; I should have had them first."
– Lois Wyse

"How many grandkids did you say you have?"

If I've heard that question once, I've heard it a hundred times. The answer is twenty-four and counting, for those who are counting. One for every letter of the alphabet, if you omit the seldom-used *X* and *Z*. Each one is special and each one is unique (even though two look exactly alike), kinda like the aforementioned letters of the alphabet. I can't imagine not having any of them. Have you ever tried to spell *catastrophic* without using an *a* and *o*? You end up with *ctstrphic*, (yep, a catastrophe).

Our grandchildren do have some things in common: love of God and family, and a genuine enjoyment of being with each other. Even though some live in different states and may not see each other for months, when they do get together, it's like they never missed a beat. For example, our "four middle girls" began sleeping on the floor in our bedroom over the Christmas holidays about sixteen years ago when everybody fit. Sixteen years and several growth spurts later, they still insist on the same sleeping arrangements, despite the obvious changes in size, and I don't mean the bedroom.

A few years ago our college grandkids at UW-Madison started a tradition of meeting every couple of weeks and having dinner together. Initially, there were five of them and it was a bit of a novelty. They designated when and where ahead of time, and rotated the responsibility for providing the meal. Given the lack of culinary prowess from some, but not all, certain meals were far less elaborate than others. But they weren't doing it for the food. Now, six years later, the practice not only continues, but flourishes. In addition to the eight current undergrads in Madison, and an occasional alum, certain close friends lobby to be "adopted" into the family so they can be a part of *famdin*.

I've also been asked many times if I have a favorite. The answer is obvious. But which one depends on the time of day, the day of the week, the week of the month, and the month of the year. Also, who last cleaned our driveway after a 4-inch snow fall.

Without grandkids, what would I have done with the hours I spent watching countless football, basketball, baseball, softball and soccer games; enjoying track and swim meets; attending dance and instrument recitals, concerts and musicals, high school and college graduations, and birthday celebrations. The reward: a hug and an acknowledgment, "Thanks for coming, Grandpa!" Priceless!

We have been blessed with a bountiful crop, so I don't really know what it would be like having only a few grandchildren. How different would Christmas or any other family get together be? Where would I find the dynamic energy that radiates through the large group and the fondness for each other; the abundance of food and other goodies, the late night conversations, the continuous games and activities, and the long good-byes? All that enthusiasm would be absent or greatly diminished. Then again, I don't know what it's like to own a luxurious New York City condominium overlooking Central Park; or drive my own Lamborghini through Europe. Different worlds, most definitely, but I'm not willing to trade.

We've had so many wonderful traditions with our grandkids: Christmas books, stories and ornaments; the recurring images of all of them scrunched together on our staircase in their pajamas on Christmas morning waiting impatiently and pleading to be released to come down to open stockings; the dreaded holiday family pictures, manners meals, whiffle ball, foosball and pickleball tournaments, football in the snow, Slammo, Kub, night games, nuke-em on the sand volleyball court, Perudo (the dice game), Texas hold 'em, Bananagrams, Boggle and so many more. Each Christmas spawns a new favorite game, and one more thing to add to the list of preferred activities.

Speaking of whiffle ball, who could forget the whiffle ball field, complete with backstop and an outfield fence, carved out of the jungle in the back five by two enterprising boys and one industrious dad? Everybody remembers the fun of pitting their team against the field in the competitive double-elimination tournament, accompanied by live play-by-play broadcast.

Grandma has a magical relationship with all her grandchildren, from tiny babies to grown adults. She always manages to do the right thing, say the right thing, or get that perfect gift. Whenever she makes something special in the kitchen, as she does quite often, it's always somebody's favorite, even though that same somebody had a different favorite of Grandma's the day before. Whoever said, "The relationship between a grandmother and grandchildren is simple; grandmas are short on criticism and long on love," knew what they were talking about.

Over the years we've had the pleasure of having individual grandkids stay with us for varying lengths of time, from one or two nights to an entire semester. We have a unique bond with these boarders. Even a few friends of our grandchildren have stayed with us while waiting on housing arrangements for school or work. Our home hasn't quite risen to the level of a youth hostel, but it defies the definition of empty nesters.

Despite all the positives, a large number of grandchildren also mean a sizable increase in the amount of angst for the grandparents. All the childhood illnesses and issues are multiplied by a multitude. Think how many earaches, colicky tummies, allergies, cuts, bruises, split heads and broken bones; let alone disappointments, distresses, emotional outbursts and perceived rejections occur in twenty-four little and not so little bodies.

One Christmas holiday, a stomach virus took up residence in our home. It raged through the family, taking no prisoners. The bug was all-inclusive and non-discriminatory; affecting male and female, adults and children. It was so insidious, some did not make it to the porcelain repository in time, especially if they were sleeping. We had empty waste baskets next to each bed and bath towels laid end to end in the upstairs hallway from all the bedrooms to the bathrooms to protect the carpet from those who couldn't make the trip without stopping. At one time we actually had a line of anxious kids waiting to get into the bathrooms so they could deposit their most recent meal.

Since we have a fairly sizable age spread between our youngest, age two, and our oldest, age 25, in any one year we may vicariously experience the joy and anxiety of the first day of preschool, middle school, high school, college, and a full-time job. Even though wedding bells have yet to sound, there are real possibilities in the immediate future. That means we could begin the cycle again with great-grandchildren.

Chapter 9: Lessons Learned

It's taken me a long time to become the person I am. – Lynn Johnson

Our background and circumstances may have influenced who we are, but we are responsible for who we become. – James Rhineheart

Reflecting back on a lifetime of experiences, I have learned some meaningful things along the way that might be worth passing on. Some were more painful than others; but all left a lasting impression.

- Never stay in a small metal boat on the water during an electric storm.
- Never carry a toilet full of water down two flights of stairs, or even one flight.
- Bathtubs produced in a metal foundry are heavy and nearly indestructible.
- Dogs are wonderful but, like children, require lots of care and attention.
- It is a good thing to be able to read the directions AND use the tools necessary to get the job done.
- Positive attitude and hard work DO make a difference.

- When you are trimming a tree, don't stop after the first branch.
- Technology is great – but oh so difficult.
- Never cut the first Christmas tree you find; you have at least an hour of searching before coming back to the original one.
- Speaking of Christmas trees, when you are trying to shorten one, don't start at the top.
- Also, anchoring a Christmas tree with fishing line avoids unplanned fallen timber.
- Time spent with children and grandchildren is its own reward.
- Always count noses before starting on any journey.
- Dreaming about greatness is easy; pursuing that dream takes hard work.
- If you want to get better, YOU must do something about it.
- Thank God for giving you each day every day.

www.ingramcontent.com/pod-product-compliance
Lightning Source LLC
Chambersburg PA
CBHW051700040426
42446CB00009B/1231